DISCOVER
Your Career

Careers If You Like

Research and Analysis

Andrea C. Nakaya

ReferencePoint Press
San Diego, CA

ReferencePoint Press®

Printed in the United States

For more information, contact:
ReferencePoint Press, Inc.
PO Box 27779
San Diego, CA 92198
www.ReferencePointPress.com

LIBRARY OF CONGRESS CATALOGING-IN-PUBLICATION DATA

Author: Andrea C. Nakaya
Title: Careers If You Like Research and Analysis
Description: San Diego, CA : ReferencePoint Press, 2026.
Series: Discover Your Career
Includes bibliographical references and index
Identifiers: LCCN 2025030157 (print) | ISBN 9781678212209 library binding | ISBN 9781678212216 ebook

For compete cataloging-in-publication data please go to www.loc.gov.

Contents

Introduction: The Importance of Research and Analysis

Thousands of different occupations involve research and analysis. Some require a college degree, while others do not. There are research jobs that require some outdoor fieldwork. Many, though, are positions within offices, labs, or libraries and likely involve sitting at a computer for long stretches of time. While some research roles are carried out in relative isolation, researchers are often part of a team working collaboratively to solve a problem or investigate a phenomenon. Researchers might help determine the best way to bring a product to market, or they could be studying the reactions of diseases to new pharmaceuticals. Others might assist investors in responding to fluctuating financial markets. Because so many career fields rely on research and analysis, there is likely to be a job that will be a good fit for those with the right talents and skills.

Helping People Understand the World and Improve Their Lives

While jobs involving research and analysis can differ significantly, they all have something in common: These occupations help people make sense of the world, make informed decisions, and solve a wide variety of problems. That makes research and analysis jobs vitally important to society. In a recent journal article, Prahlada N. Basavanthappa, a doctor at Basaveshwara Medical College and Hospital in India, writes, "Research holds a pivotal role in human civilization. It serves as an instrument to enhance our understanding of the world. . . . From the intricacies of the human body to the complex interplay of global economies, research gives us insight and equips us with knowledge to make informed decisions in various fields such as medicine, business, and policy." In addition, he says that research drives innovation, explaining, "The societal problems that we encounter are rarely simple, and research provides the vital tools for addressing and solving these complex issues. Its influence extends to economic growth, especially in Research and Development (R and D)–driven industries where new products and services are born out of rigorous research."[1]

Examples of Jobs That Involve Research and Analysis

For students interested in a job that involves coming up with innovative solutions to problems, a science-based job may be a good option. For example, climate scientists collect and analyze data on climate change and discover strategies for reducing the impacts of things like extreme heat. Epidemiologists are scientists who focus on patterns of viral or bacterial infection to find ways to stop the spread of diseases like measles. From police detectives to geologists, many professions utilize research and analysis in gathering and studying information to solve current or potential problems and puzzles.

Research and analysis jobs can also improve people's lives. For instance, psychologists study human behavior so that they can teach people how to achieve better mental health and cope with stressful events. Food scientists analyze food and work to improve its safety, quality, or nutritional value. There are also jobs focused on improving the health of nature. For example, a forester oversees forests and develops management plans that ensure the future health of woodlands while accommodating human recreational needs.

Research and analysis also help people know what has happened in the past to build a better future. Historians study events and artifacts and share their findings so that humanity can understand and learn from the past. Journalists and political analysts also examine past events, looking at patterns that might provide a better understanding of what is happening in the present.

Research and analysis also help people make informed decisions about what to do in the future. For instance, urban planners analyze land use to develop plans for building sustainable and functional communities. Actuaries use mathematical analysis to help companies and organizations assess financial risks and take action to reduce those risks. Sports data analysts collect data about the performances of athletes and teams, such as game statistics and information about player health, and look for patterns and trends that can help coaches improve outcomes.

In-Demand Skills

Because researchers are important in so many ways, surveys consistently find that they provide some of the most in-demand skills in the job market. For instance, in the World Economic Forum's *Future of Jobs Report 2025*, the authors state, "Analytical thinking remains the most sought-after core skill among employers, with seven out of 10 companies considering it as essential in 2025."[2] As technology and job markets change over time, the job skills that employers need also change. However, most experts believe that research and analysis are fundamental job skills that will always be needed.

Data Scientist

Every year the software company Domo releases a report called *Data Never Sleeps* that details what happens on the internet every day. Its 2024 edition shows a staggering amount of activity: Every minute people send 2.43 million snaps, conduct 5.9 million Google searches, and upload 500 hours of video on YouTube, among other things. All this activity creates data about users, including their likes and dislikes, who their friends are, and their online activity. Data scientists are professionals who collect and analyze these types of data.

Although industries have mined data for more than a century, the title of data scientist is a relatively new one, arising roughly twenty-five years ago alongside the growth of digital tech giants and e-commerce corporations. Today it has become one of the most in-demand professions in the world. Data scientists use the insights they get from their analysis to help businesses of all kinds get a better understanding of their customers and figure out ways to improve their business practices. In a blog post, the New York Institute of Technology explains just how important data scientists are: "In modern industries, data has become the lifeblood that fuels progress and innovation. . . . Successful data

At a Glance

Number of Jobs
About 202,900

Pay
About $112,000 in 2024

Educational Requirements
Strong coding, math, and computer skills

Personal Qualities
Analytical, good communicator

Working Conditions
In an office or working remotely, usually with regular hours

Future Job Outlook
Growth of 36 percent through 2033

analysis can help unearth critical insights about your business, such as how to streamline business operations, predict customer behavior, and reduce waste. This puts data scientists, and others who can effectively wield data, in high demand."[3]

What Does a Data Scientist Do?

In the digital age, data scientists collect and analyze torrents of facts, figures, opinions, and other bits of information. They sift through the numerous data points to find trends, relationships, or other types of patterns, and they share their findings with other people, who often lack such technical expertise. Some people liken this job to detective work or treasure hunting. In an online post, tech company Xaltius says, "In a world overflowing with information, data science is the key to uncovering its hidden treasures. It's like being a digital Indiana Jones, armed with algorithms and statistics, on a quest to unravel the mysteries buried within terabytes of data. But forget dusty tombs and booby traps—the thrill of data science lies in unearthing insights that can change the world."[4]

The process usually starts with research. Data scientists need to figure out what kind of data is available to them for the specific task they are trying to accomplish, and then they need to gather that data. For example, a data scientist trying to figure out how a company can improve its products might use data from user reviews to understand what people like and do not like. Data scientists often work with very large datasets, which can come from several different places. Sometimes, they use web-scraping tools, which are programs that automatically collect information from websites. Data scientists might also access large databases owned by government agencies, academic institutions, big companies, or other types of organizations. After gathering the data, they need to do something called "cleaning," which means getting rid of errors, duplicates, and inaccurate data so that what remains is clean and ready to use.

Looking for Patterns

"We try to identify the patterns from really big data. So, for example in retail, you do online shopping, or you'll look at house pricings in real estate, or if you want a forecast of stock price in the next three years. . . . What we're trying to do is to identify patterns in data. Trying to distill very unstructured data and make it to an understandable format so we can see . . . if we can extract any pattern or we can identify any relationship among various factors."

—Ping Mamiya Chao, data scientist at Oracle

Quoted in Oracle Careers Editorial Team, "Data Science at Oracle: A Thriving Career Path," *Oracle Careers Blog*, January 18, 2024. https://blogs.oracle.com.

For analysis, data scientists rely on computer algorithms—that is, sets of instructions—that can quickly analyze large amounts of data; something that would be impossible for a person to do alone. Data scientists often work with existing algorithms within their field, but if the program does not produce the needed results, these professionals might write new code to test new algorithms specific to the task.

After analyzing their data, data scientists share their findings with other people, such as clients or employers. To make their findings easier to understand, they typically utilize data visualization. This means using computer software to create visual representations of their findings, such as maps, charts, and graphs. With these aids, it can be easier for even those not trained in data science to spot patterns.

A Typical Workday

Entry-level data scientists often spend most of their time gathering and processing data. After they gain more experience, they will typically be able to focus more on analysis and presentation of their findings. People who work at smaller companies may need to handle all these steps themselves regardless of their level of

In meetings with clients, colleagues, or company executives, data scientists explain their data analysis and findings. They use charts and graphs to show patterns in the data, making their findings easier for others to understand.

experience. When it comes to sharing their findings, they might need to attend meetings, either in person or virtually on a platform like Zoom.

Data scientists also need to spend time keeping themselves up-to-date with new technology in this field. Data science technology changes quickly, so this is an important part of the job. Data scientist Egor Howell explains that this is one of the things he enjoys about being a data scientist. He says, "As a data scientist, I get to be right at the forefront of the latest tech trends. . . . There is always something new and exciting to learn, which I love! So, if you want to constantly learn new skills and apply them, then data science may be a career you would be interested in."[5]

Education and Training

Most data scientists have at least a bachelor's degree, and many have a more advanced degree such as a master's degree or even a doctorate. There is not one specific degree needed to prepare for this career; instead, data scientists come from many different backgrounds. Common degrees are in STEM fields, including computer science, statistics, mathematics, business, and engineering. Some people also take shorter courses like boot camps or certificate classes to master programming languages or data visualization applications. These types of classes usually take only a few months to complete.

No matter their educational degree, data scientists need to study mathematics. The Bureau of Labor Statistics (BLS) suggests starting early. It says, "High school students interested in becoming data scientists should take classes in subjects such as linear algebra, calculus, and probability and statistics."[6] Mathematics classes should continue through college. However, while data science does involve a lot of math, data scientist Alireza Dibazar advises that potential data scientists should not be deterred if they do not have all the math skills right away, because other talents are also needed for this job. For instance, he says that curiosity and critical thinking are important, too. "While a background in mathematics can be helpful," he says, "data scientists can develop their mathematical skills over time. What's essential is a strong willingness to learn and a passion for problem-solving."[7]

Skills and Personality

This job requires a combination of technical skills, like mathematics, and "soft" skills, which are personality traits and interpersonal skills. One of the most important technical skills in this field is coding, since computer code is used both for obtaining data and for analyzing it. For instance, the algorithms that analyze data are created with code. Python and R are two of the most popular coding languages used in data science. Professionals in this field also need fluency in several different software applications, which are used to analyze data and to turn it into visuals so that it can be better understood. Popular applications include Power BI and Tableau.

When it comes to the soft skills, data scientists need problem-solving and analytical skills so that they can conduct research and analyze their findings. Creativity is also helpful for solving problems like how to fix an algorithm that is not working. Since part of this job is communicating findings, data scientists need to be skilled communicators, too. This is helpful when they are called on to explain technical concepts to nontechnical audiences.

Workplace, Employers, and Pay

Most data scientists work in an office. Travel is not usually a significant part of this job. Data scientists work for a wide variety of employers since many different companies have a need for experts who can analyze data. Employers include tech companies, government agencies, health care companies, financial firms, retail companies, universities, and other research institutions. It is often possible to do this job remotely, and a significant number of data scientists do so.

The average salary in this field is high. According to the BLS, the median annual salary for a data scientist is about $112,000. This is more than double the average wage for all jobs in the United States, which is approximately $49,000. BLS data shows that large metropolitan areas like Los Angeles, Seattle, San Francisco, and New York City tend to have the highest pay.

What Is the Future Outlook for Data Scientists?

Data science is the fourth-highest career on the list of Fastest Growing Occupations published by the BLS. Over the next decade, the agency predicts that employment of data scientists will grow by 36 percent, which is much faster than the average US job growth rate of only 4 percent. It anticipates more than twenty thousand job openings each year over that time. It ex-

The Ability to Work in Many Different Industries

"As data scientists progress in their careers, they often specialise in a specific area, honing their skills and expertise within a particular industry. This helps them become more valuable later on and carve out their own niche in the market. . . . As a data scientist, you can work in loads of different industries during your career. So far, I have worked in insurance and e-commerce, and I have only been working for 3 years! However, to become a real specialist, you need to find and stick to one industry you love."

—Egor Howell, data scientist and machine learning engineer

Egor Howell, "Behind the Scenes: Explaining My Work as a Data Scientist," Medium, May 24, 2024. https://medium.com.

plains that this growth is being driven by an expanding need to use data for making decisions, stating,

> The volume of data available and the potential uses for that data will increase. . . . As a result, organizations will likely need more data scientists to mine and analyze the large amounts of information and data collected. Data scientists' analysis will help organizations to make informed decisions and improve their business processes, to design and develop new products, and to better market their products.[8]

Find Out More

Academic Data Science Alliance

https://academicdatascience.org

This organization of academic professionals works to advance best practices in the field of data science and its incorporation of artificial intelligence. Its Slack community contains internship opportunities and job postings, and its website has information about community data science events.

American Statistical Association (ASA)

www.amstat.org

The goal of the ASA is to promote the practice of statistical analysis, including within the field of data science. Its website contains many different educational resources, such as guidelines and reports specifically designed for students. It also has career resources, including salary information.

Institute for Operations Research and the Management Sciences

www.informs.org

This association supports professionals who work in data science and related fields. Its website has a variety of educational resources, including its *Analytics Magazine*, which has articles about how data analysis is used. Its career center contains job listings and a variety of career advice articles.

Financial Analyst

Knowing how to manage money is an important skill for anyone. It can help people make smart spending choices, avoid debt, and save money for future needs. It can also be a way to make more money, through investing. The investment company Fidelity explains, "Investing is putting your money to work in a stock, bond, mutual fund, exchange-traded fund (ETF), or other financial instruments with the potential of making a profit." While investing can be risky, it can also be very lucrative. Fidelity insists, "Investing is a powerful way to help your money grow."[9] Financial analysts are investment specialists. They collect and analyze financial information and help individuals or businesses make smart decisions about how to invest their money.

At a Glance

Number of Jobs
About 404,800

Pay
About $101,000 in 2024

Educational Requirements
Bachelor's degree in economics, accounting, finance, or related field

Personal Qualities
Detail oriented, analytical, good with numbers, strong communicator

Working Conditions
In office; may travel to meet with clients

Future Job Outlook
Growth of 9 percent through 2033

What Does a Financial Analyst Do?

Financial analysts look at many different types of financial information, such as company financial documents, historical reports about the economy, stock market information, and opinions from other experts in the finance industry. They analyze all these resources and try to predict the least risky and most profitable investment strategies for their clients. The Institute of Management Accountants, an association of accounting and finance professionals, describes this job as a process of taking lots of small details and figuring out how they all relate to one another. Its website asserts, "If the idea of analyzing 'big picture' trends sounds like something you're interested in, then a job as a financial analyst may be just what you're looking for. It's a role that's great for people who like to take a whole bunch of data, figure out the story it's telling, and then make decisions that will help their company get the most bang for their investment buck."[10]

People who work in this field often specialize in a specific type of financial analysis and, depending on their interest, can have one of several job titles. For example, a risk analyst is a financial analyst who focuses on identifying and limiting potential risks to a company. An equity research analyst specializes in making investment recommendations for publicly traded companies. Other job titles include fund manager, hedge fund analyst, securities analyst, and investment analyst—each with its own area of expertise.

Financial analysts spend a lot of time gathering and evaluating financial data. They use computer applications like Microsoft Excel to organize, analyze, and present large datasets. For instance, Excel allows them to calculate a company's asset value or growth rate and categorize complex information for easier interpretation. These insights help inform recommendations on investment strategies.

Companies often rely on the findings of financial analysts to make major financial decisions. Kevin Ha, a financial associate analyst at Canadian Tire Corporation, says that this potential to influence what people do is one of his favorite things about this job. He attests, "It excites me when analytics come to life and provide insights that drive change."[11]

Mistakes and Problems Are Part of the Job

"This job is not stress free! Our job is all about making the expected value of our actions positive—however, no one can have a 100% hit [success] rate. There will be trades that lose money or ideas that don't work out, and sometimes we need to manage our emotions well when things do not go our way. I do think being able to learn from mistakes and move on quickly is an acquired skill that's very important for my continued growth and for not limiting myself to the past."

—Carina, analyst at Citadel Securities

Quoted in "Carina," Prosple, 2025. https://au.prosple.com.

A Typical Workday

Pam Chang is an equities analyst at hedge fund firm Citadel. She manages her clients' stock portfolios and spends much of her day keeping track of what is happening in financial markets. She says, "I wake up and check my phone to go through the news and see what happened overnight in the markets and with the stocks I cover. I also have a quick look . . . to see if I have any communications from my colleagues in our global offices, or whether any new viewpoints on my stocks have emerged while I was sleeping." According to Chang, her plans can change significantly if there are unexpected market changes. She says, "This can be the best and worst time of my work day—best because you never know what the market will throw at you, and it can be very exciting to interpret implications from news of the day. . . . I say it's the worst because sometimes you have to rip up your daily schedule and reprioritize depending on what's taking place."[12]

In addition to collecting and analyzing information, financial analysts create reports of their findings and offer recommendations. Typically, they use these reports to explain their insights to people who are not experts in financial analysis. They also meet with colleagues, managers, or clients to discuss financial strategies. For instance, Ha says that about 20 percent of his workday is devoted to meetings. Entry-level financial analysts commonly spend a lot of their time on the research part of the job. As they gain experience, they gain responsibility and are likely to spend more time on analysis and reporting.

Education and Training

Most entry-level financial analysis positions require a bachelor's degree, and some employers prefer a master's degree. Financial analysts need to learn about economics, accounting, and business. Acquiring a business, finance, or economics degree is the most common way to enter this field. Some types of financial analysts need to be licensed by the Financial Industry Regulatory Authority. Licensing requirements are designed to make sure that analysts treat their customers fairly and ethically. There are licenses for conducting business and for selling different types of financial products like stocks or bonds. For example, to conduct business in a specific state, a financial advisor must obtain a Series 63 license, which is earned by passing an exam covering that state's financial laws and regulations. Acquiring a Series 7 license, on the other hand, allows a financial analyst to sell investment products like stocks and bonds.

In this profession, education is ongoing. Financial analysts need to regularly devote time to staying up-to-date on financial trends, new technology, and regulatory changes. The Association for Financial Professionals insists, "The world of finance is always evolving, so continuous learning is crucial to your success." It advises, "Ways to continue growing . . . include conversations with peers, professional conferences and webinars, and certifications."[13]

Skills and Personality

Since financial analysts work with numbers every day, they need strong math skills and should be detail oriented to ensure accuracy

Financial analysts gather and evaluate financial data. They develop recommendations on investment strategies with the aid of computer applications and spreadsheets.

in their work. They also need analytical and problem-solving skills, which will help them find patterns and trends, draw conclusions, and resolve challenges. Challenges are common in this profession. As the Association for Financial Professionals explains, "Very few plans play out exactly as envisioned." It explains that financial analysts need to be ready to respond to challenges and have a backup plan ready. It says, "While the finance analyst is putting together the expected outcomes, they also need to think about the other possible outcomes."[14]

People who work in this field need to explain their findings and recommendations to clients, managers, business owners, and others who likely do not have the same level of financial expertise. Therefore, they need excellent written and verbal communication skills and should be comfortable explaining data and

There Is Always Something to Learn

"My role involves helping clients analyze their business in detail, prepare business plans, financial models, and information memoranda that would help our clients facilitate capital raising, strategic planning, and decision making. I also build business intelligence solutions to help clients keep tabs on business performance. So far, it has been challenging and exciting. No two businesses are entirely the same so there's always something new to learn."

—Habeeb Olusanya, financial analyst at Leonine Investment Services

Quoted in Leonine Investment Services, "How I Transitioned into Finance: Habeeb Olusanya, Financial Analyst at Leonine," Medium, June 30, 2021. https://medium.com.

offering advice to both individuals and larger groups of people. Olu Sonola, a certified financial analyst and the head of US economic research at Fitch Ratings in New York, insists, "The ability to translate technical skills into easily understandable concepts is crucial. Communication is one skill that many people tend to take for granted. But . . . you have to be able to distill and synthesize a lot of information. Your writing needs to be understood by pretty much anybody."[15]

Workplace, Employers, and Pay

Most financial analysts work in an office. Sometimes, travel is required, especially to meet with clients. Some financial analysts work remotely, but this job typically involves a lot of interaction with other people, so off-site opportunities are less common. Many financial analysts are employed by fiscal institutions like banks, insurance companies, and money management companies. Others work for large corporations, nonprofit organizations, and government agencies. Some may even serve regulatory agencies such as the US Securities and Exchange Commission, which is a federal agency that regulates the securities market.

Pay in this field is relatively high. According to the Bureau of Labor Statistics (BLS), the median salary for a financial analyst is about $101,000. The agency reports that large financial centers such as New York City, Los Angeles, and Chicago have the most jobs in this field.

What Is the Future Outlook for Financial Analysts?

Because there will always be businesses that need investment advice, the outlook for jobs in financial analysis is positive. The BLS notes, "Demand for financial analysts generally increases with overall economic activity,"[16] which means that there are likely to be more job opportunities when the economy is growing. Overall, the BLS anticipates growth of 9 percent for financial analysts through 2033, which is more than double the average US job growth rate and equals more than thirty thousand new jobs per year. *U.S. News & World Report* ranks financial advisor at number two on its list of Best Business Jobs while also including it in its index of 20 Careers with the Most Job Security.

Find Out More

Association for Financial Professionals (AFP)

www.afponline.org

The AFP is a professional certification body, but its website has a variety of educational resources, including a section devoted to financial analysis. Visitors can also find information about financial certifications and peruse a career hub with job postings and résumé and interview tips.

Financial Industry Regulatory Authority (FINRA)

www.finra.org

FINRA is a self-regulatory organization that oversees licensing for financial professionals. Its website has information about licensing and regulations within the securities industry. There is also a "Frequently Asked Questions" section.

National Association of Insurance and Financial Advisors

https://belong.naifa.org

The National Association of Insurance and Financial Advisors is an organization for financial service professionals. Its website has many different educational resources, including journal articles and webinars.

Wildlife Biologist

Growing up, Zaara Kidwai was not exactly sure what type of job she wanted to do, but she always had a strong interest in nature. During summers, she would visit her grandmother's house, where she enjoyed seeing the local wildlife. She explains, "I was curious to know about them, and I would get very excited on seeing something new, be it a bird or a butterfly or a deer." She now works as a wildlife biologist for Montana's Department of Fish, Wildlife & Parks. She has found that this job is a good way to continue to learn more about the natural environment. Though she warns that the job often involves hard work in challenging conditions, it is very fulfilling. She says, "You learn so much about the environment around you in this field, by getting outside of your comfort zone with not enough compensation. You have to be really involved in order to be a part of this beautiful world. But once you have got the taste for it, you will never be satisfied with learning about it, and always want more."[17]

At a Glance

Number of Jobs
About 18,800

Pay
About $72,000 in 2024

Educational Requirements
Bachelor's degree in zoology or wildlife biology

Personal Qualities
Attention to detail, critical thinking, curiosity, physical stamina

Working Conditions
Both in the field and in the office; irregular hours and challenging conditions are common

Future Job Outlook
Growth of 4 percent through 2033

What Does a Wildlife Biologist Do?

Wildlife biologists study animals and the way those animals interact with their environments, and they come up with ways to help manage and protect animals, especially from human encroachment. This job involves a lot of research. Wildlife biologists observe animals to better understand key aspects of their lives, including population size, diet, reproduction, and interactions with other species. They often collect specimens of blood, hair, feathers, or feces to study. They might also gather environmental samples like water or soil to learn more about the animals' habitat.

By gaining a better understanding of a particular animal, wildlife biologists learn how to keep that animal and its ecosystem healthy. In many cases, they identify threats—such as predators, human intrusion, or disease—and try to mitigate their impacts on the wildlife of a region.

Another part of the job of a wildlife biologist is to share insights with other people. Some wildlife biologists do this by interacting with the public. For instance, they might present information at educational events or teach workshops. Many write research papers or reports to share with government agencies and policymakers. Matt Lau, a wildlife biologist for the National Park Service, says that the opportunity to educate other people is one of the things he likes about his job. He says that he feels like he is increasing awareness about environmental protection, stating, "Being able to connect people with science is something that I really enjoy. Sharing my love for science and conservation is something that I look forward to every day."[18]

A Typical Workday

Wildlife biologists work in many different settings and do many different jobs. For most people though, the job involves two main types of activities: fieldwork and writing up their findings. When it comes to fieldwork, most wildlife biologists caution that the job often involves physical work that can be both difficult and unpleasant. Writing on the Maine Department of Inland Fisheries &

Learning How to Deal with Challenges

"There are a lot of challenges in this field and some are tougher than the others. It is all about how you deal with it at the time, in a remote area, with no cell network. All the great things that we see on television about wildlife are extremely glamorized, and they don't show the things that happen in the field. Sometimes you have to wait hours for your target animal to come to the spot or do what you want it to do. Sometimes you don't see the animal at all, even with the radio collar. Sometimes the challenge is having no work in the field but only paperwork."

—Zaara Kidwai, wildlife biologist with the Montana Department of Fish, Wildlife & Parks

Quoted in Interview Portal, "Wildlife Biologist Interview," June 23, 2023. https://theinterviewportal.com.

Wildlife blog, wildlife outreach biologist Lauren McPherson warns, "While the unique experiences occasionally produce envious photos snuggling a bear cub during a den visit, a moose that's been immobilized to safely relocate it, or a banded peregrine chick that closely resembles a pile of mashed potatoes with a beak, the reality of the job can be much more challenging than the images lead on." She explains that she often has long days outside in difficult terrain and harsh temperatures. For example, she says, "Capturing and surveying for bunnies, New England cottontail (NEC) specifically, might sound 'easy,' but it isn't for the faint of heart. . . . These little rabbits live in areas of extreme thickets and thorns, making it next to impossible to push and pull your way through vines that hook onto your clothing, scratch your skin, and pierce through your layers, all during cold, windy, winter days."[19]

The writing side of the job can also be more difficult than many people realize. Stephanie Manka has been a wildlife biologist for twenty years. She stresses that this job requires a commitment to research and writing, which may seem less glamorous than

A wildlife biologist in Alaska carries a tranquilized female lynx to an area where she will be evaluated and tagged. Fieldwork such as this helps these professionals gain a better understanding of animals and their habitat needs.

observing or handling cute animals. She says, "When people hear 'study wildlife' they usually visualize images of scientists watching animals in the wild or collecting some kind of sample. While this is part of it, they don't think of all of the hours spent afterwards analyzing data, writing up results, or writing the next grant to get funding."[20] Not only is there a lot of writing, she says, but much of it needs to be at a high academic level.

Education and Training

Because this job demands a sophisticated understanding of the environment, the habits and nature of animals, and academic or journal writing, a wildlife biologist must possess a relatively high level of education. Wildlife biologists typically take university courses in biology, anatomy, and ecology. They often need to understand math and statistics so that they can conduct data analysis. Most graduate from college with a bachelor's degree in zoology, wildlife biology, biology, or natural resources. Higher-level positions—especially research positions—may require a master's or doctoral degree.

Wildlife biologists also need to learn how to do fieldwork, which is a major part of the job. They can start gaining fieldwork experience while they are still in school—for example, by volunteering or finding an internship. McPherson advises volunteering for fieldwork early in the educational process. She says, "Going along with a biologist in the field can help you acquire greater understanding of the field work, whether or not you'd enjoy the work, and helps you build relationships and skills early on."[21]

Skills and Personality

This job entails spending a lot of time observing nature, and wildlife biologists need to be good at paying attention to small details so that they do not miss anything important when managing animal populations. They also need critical-thinking and problem-solving skills so that they can analyze their findings and come up with solutions to threats to these populations. In addition to simply observing, wildlife biologists ask lots of questions about what they see, so curiosity is an asset in this field. Finally, communication skills are important since this job usually involves explaining their findings to other people.

To work outdoors, they need to be physically fit and strong enough to carry heavy equipment over long distances. Rather than trekking through the forest, Lau works along a California beach observing breeds of plover, a migratory bird. He says that his work is still physically demanding. He explains, "It's definitely very hard work, labor-wise. I mean I'm walking long distances on the beach almost every day between March until September, during the plover season. . . . It's difficult in the moment but afterwards, it's very rewarding."[22]

Workplace Settings

Wildlife biologists work in a variety of settings. The US Forest Service states, "Forest Service biologists work in all types of environments—offices and mountains, deserts and wetlands, forests and prairies—we have it all."[23] Wildlife biologists might need to travel to remote locations and stay there for extended periods of time. They might also have to spend time in many different types of weather, risking injury or illness. When conducting this fieldwork, wildlife biologists are likely to follow irregular work hours. For example, if they are observing a nocturnal animal, they may have to work at night.

In many cases, this job involves working as part of a team. For example, a wildlife biologist might travel to a research location as part of a research team that includes other environmental experts like zoologists, hydrologists, or environmental scientists. Alternatively, they might conduct fieldwork alone but then meet up with team members at the end to discuss their findings.

Once out of the field, wildlife biologists may conduct research in offices in front of computers, or they might examine animals or environmental samples in a laboratory. There also may be trips to other institutions or libraries to gather information and consult with colleagues.

Employers and Pay

Wildlife biologists can work for government agencies like the US Fish and Wildlife Service or the National Park Service, nonprofit organizations like the World Wildlife Fund, zoos or aquariums, museums, or universities. According to the Bureau of Labor Statistics (BLS), about 18,800 wildlife biologists and zoologists work in the United States, and 67 percent are employed by govern-

Becoming a Voice for Animals

"I very clearly remember as a young child . . . I really could see that if animals had a voice, people would not treat them the way they do. I swore to myself as a child that if I was ever able to find my voice, that I would be their voice. I would be there for them. I'm not saying that's the only reason I took the path I did, but it's been in my mind for my entire life, trying to give back to these animals, who want nothing more than to live their own lives the best that they can."

—Alan Rabinowitz, wildlife biologist and founder of the big cat conservation organization Panthera

Quoted in Krista Tippett, "We Are All Wildlife," On Being, August 16, 2018. https://onbeing.org.

ment agencies. The average annual salary for this occupation, as reported by the BLS, is about $72,000. The BLS finds that government agencies generally pay more than colleges and universities or social advocacy organizations.

What Is the Future Outlook for Wildlife Biologists?

The BLS predicts a continued need for wildlife biologists in the future, with a projected growth rate of 4 percent through 2033. That rate is comparable to the average growth across all occupations in the United States and equates to approximately fifteen hundred job openings for wildlife biologists each year. The BLS explains that many future jobs will be related to climate change, stating, "Some zoologists and wildlife biologists are expected to be needed to help combat the loss of biodiversity caused by human activities, as well as to research climate-driven ecosystem changes. These workers also may be needed to develop and implement conservation plans to reduce threats to animals and protect natural resources."[24]

Find Out More

Association of Zoos & Aquariums (AZA)

www.aza.org

The AZA is a nonprofit organization supporting zoos and aquariums. Its website contains many different resources about conservation and animal care. There are also job postings and a career center, which contains information about different types of jobs and how to prepare for them, as well as internship resources.

Wildlife Society

https://wildlife.org

The Wildlife Society is an organization that empowers wildlife agency professionals by providing opportunities for learning, networking, and career development. In addition to a variety of professional resources, its website contains sections for students, including information about careers in wildlife, as well as a list of schools that offer education in this field.

Zoological Association of America (ZAA)

https://zooassociation.org

The ZAA is a nonprofit organization that promotes conservation and responsible wildlife management. Its website houses a variety of professional development resources such as webinars and its magazine, the *ZAA Journal*. There is also a job board with postings for positions around the United States.

Forensic Science Technician

In most cases when a crime is committed, physical evidence is left at the scene. It can be something obvious, such as a dead body or a weapon, or not so obvious, such as footprints, clothing fibers, or hair. The National Institute of Justice explains that this evidence often plays an important role in helping law enforcement officers understand what happened and find the perpetrator of the crime. The institute's website explains, "Oftentimes, evidence tells a story and helps an investigator re-create the crime scene and establish the sequence of events." In fact, the institute adds, physical evidence can be more reliable than witnesses: "Physical evidence is objective and when documented, collected, and preserved properly may be the only way to reliably place or link someone with a crime scene."[25] Forensic science technicians gather and analyze physical evidence, and their work aids investigators in solving many criminal cases.

At a Glance

Number of Jobs
About 18,600

Pay
About $67,000 in 2024

Educational Requirements
Bachelor's degree in forensic science or a related field

Personal Qualities
Attention to detail, problem-solving, communication, emotional resilience

Working Conditions
At crime scenes and in laboratories; crime scenes may be disturbing

Future Job Outlook
Growth of 14 percent through 2033

What Does a Forensic Science Technician Do?

By collecting and examining evidence from crime scenes, forensic science technicians assist law enforcement professionals in determining when and how a crime occurred and what suspects may be linked to the scene. They take photos of and document the evidence from the location, and they collect fingerprints, bodily fluids, weapons, tire imprints, paint chips, glass shards, soil, vegetation, and other evidence to help investigators create a plausible scenario to explain how a crime was committed. They examine their evidence in a laboratory using a variety of tools and methods. For example, they might analyze hair or bodily fluids under a microscope, or they might use a computer to compare deoxyribonucleic acid (DNA) evidence to medical records. Technological advances in this field mean that forensic science technicians often use a lot of advanced scientific techniques to analyze evidence. For example, they can use software for facial reconstruction from skeletal remains, or they can match fragments of broken glass from a crime scene to makers or sellers of that glass. Some forensic science technicians specialize in either crime scene or laboratory work. They may also specialize in specific types of analysis, like ballistics or DNA sampling.

Forensic science technicians also prepare reports to present their findings to law enforcement professionals or lawyers. In addition, they may need to testify as expert witnesses in court. Antoinette T. Campbell, a forensic scientist in Philadelphia who specializes in analyzing drug evidence, says that this is one of the parts of the job that she likes best. She says, "You see how it all really works. You have a big responsibility to make sure that when you're analyzing evidence, you're doing the right thing. You're taking your time and you're not being sloppy. You're taking it seriously, because this is somebody's life on the line."[26]

Reality crime shows like *CSI: Crime Scene Investigation* have become popular on television for their portrayal of analysts gathering evidence at crime scenes. However, many forensic science technicians complain that these types of shows do not accurately depict the work. Forensic scientist Rebecca Learned says, "Is it

Helping Ensure Justice

"[The best thing about being a forensic scientist is] the ability to use your scientific knowledge and skills to put pieces together that can lead to a fair and prompt administration of justice. Every time that I open a case, there is communication between the evidence and the scientist. We let the evidence become the 'mute witness' that can help decipher clues about what, when or how things may have evolved in a criminal event."

—Tatiana Trejos, associate professor of forensic science at West Virginia University

Quoted in Jake Stump, "The Last Word," *WVU Magazine*, February 2024. https://magazine.wvu.edu.

as glamorous and fast-paced as some of the fictional TV crime shows portray it to be? No. It can be tedious, messy, sometimes smelly, and there are always plenty of reports to write." However, Learned and many others also stress that while many television shows get details wrong, this job is often both exciting and fulfilling. Learned says, "At its core, being a forensic scientist involves the search for truth about a crime, whether that means helping to catch a criminal or helping to eliminate an innocent person as a suspect. I thoroughly enjoy what I do."[27]

Education and Training

Most forensic science technicians have a bachelor's degree in forensic science or a related field like chemistry, biology, or physical science. Professor Sreetharan Kanthaswamy teaches forensic science at Arizona State University's School of Interdisciplinary Forensics. His advice to students who want to pursue a career in this field is that they need a strong scientific knowledge base. He explains, "Students must realize that forensic science is an interdisciplinary field that integrates biology, chemistry, and other sciences to reconstruct crime scenes effectively. Therefore, they need to have a sound scientific background to be successful forensic analysts." Not only that, but he stresses that ongoing education is important to success: "Students should stay updated on the latest technologies and approaches and embrace the hard work and dedication needed for the field."[28]

In addition to education, forensic science technicians usually receive training on the job. The Bureau of Labor Statistics (BLS) explains that this is how novices learn to do things like collecting and processing evidence correctly. It says, "Newly hired crime scene technicians may be supervised by experienced workers, who instruct them in procedures for collecting and documenting evidence."[29] The BLS says that this type of training usually takes less than a year.

Aspiring forensic science technicians should also be mindful of their public record. On its "Career Outlook" page for the forensic science graduate program, the University of California, Davis, explains that people who work in forensic science may need to present sworn testimony in court, so there is likely to be a detailed background check and maybe even a polygraph as part of the hiring process. The program says, "The criteria used to evaluate an applicant varies from agency to agency, but many agencies examine criminal history (felony and misdemeanor), recreational drug use and credit history. . . . If you are seeking employment in forensic science do not use drugs, do not break the law, and do not have bad credit."[30]

Skills and Personality

Attention to detail is important in this job, since even the smallest details can be crucial to solving a case. Forensic science technicians also need strong analytical skills so that they can use the evidence they have collected to figure out what might have happened at the crime scene. Forensic scientist Michael Howard says that this makes the job interesting. "What I enjoy most about forensic science is the problem solving," he asserts. "You look at the evidence to see what it's telling you."[31] Communication is also important. Forensic scientists need to be able to explain complex findings in a way that can be understood by nonexperts. Sometimes, they must do so in court.

Forensic science technicians may encounter disturbing details at crime scenes, so it is also beneficial to be emotionally resilient in this career, with the ability to stay professional even in traumatic situations. When asked how he handles the stress of his job, Howard says that forensic science experts often develop unique ways of coping: "A lot of it is talking with the people you deal with every day. In forensics we often develop a warped sense of humor; we find humor in grotesque things. Forensic folks together will laugh about stuff that would horrify people outside the field. You build your own defenses, and vent it at work."[32]

Employers and Pay

According to the BLS, the median salary for a forensic science technician is about $67,000. Most forensic science technicians are employed by the government, with approximately 60 percent working for local governments and 27 percent for state governments. They work in several different settings, including crime laboratories, police departments, and medical examiners' offices. Many work a regular nine-to-five schedule; however, they may be on call at any time to respond to crime scenes. Some positions also require occasional travel.

Roxanne works in the field of forensic science. In an interview, she explains that what can be achieved within the daily schedule is very different than what is portrayed on television. For example, she says that gathering and analyzing evidence is usually a lot more time-consuming and tedious than many people think. "The processes take really long, it's not all wrapped up on a 30-minute show," says Roxanne. "It can take weeks to look at an item of

The Importance of Environmental Evidence

"A crime scene can happen anywhere; the perpetrator of a crime cannot stop the environment leaving traces of itself on them, nor the perpetrator leaving traces of themselves on the environment. The environment—and the organisms associated with it—can be the key of the investigation in order to identify place, time and people involved in a crime. . . . A big challenge of my job is that the environment is in continuous evolution and many environments have not been studied before a crime happens within it. It can be extremely challenging to discern between evidence that is simply part of the environment or is there because of the crime."

—Paola Magni, forensic scientist who specializes in the analysis of insects and other creatures to solve crimes

Quoted in Murdoch University News, "What's It like to Be a Forensic Scientist," August 15, 2018. www.murdoch.edu.au.

evidence. A lot of the biggest misconceptions have to do with the crime scenes. They can take forever to process."[33] Kanthaswamy agrees. He says, "Forensic science requires patience, collaboration, and meticulous attention to detail. It's not like TV shows where crimes are solved in 45 minutes."[34]

What Is the Future Outlook for Forensic Science Technicians?

The BLS predicts that the employment of forensic science technicians will grow by 14 percent through 2033, which is much faster than the average US job growth rate of 4 percent. It anticipates about twenty-seven hundred job openings each year. The agency explains that there are several reasons for this growing demand. One is simply that state and local governments need these experts to help process the many open criminal investigations. Additionally, technological advances in forensic science are making this field more useful than ever before. The BLS explains, "Scientific and technological advances are expected to increase the availability, reliability, and usefulness of objective forensic information used as evidence in trials. As a result, more forensic science technicians will be needed to provide forensics information to law enforcement agencies and courts."[35]

Find Out More

American Academy of Forensic Sciences

www.aafs.org

The American Academy of Forensic Sciences is a professional organization that supports education and leadership in this field. Its website has a variety of fact sheets on forensic science, a listing of schools with forensics programs, and current job postings.

International Association for Identification

www.theiai.org

The International Association for Identification is a membership association for forensic professionals. Its website has information about conferences, job openings, and internship opportunities. There is also a list of links to other forensic organizations.

International Crime Scene Investigators Association

https://icsia.wildapricot.org

This organization supports professionals who process crime scenes. Its website contains trade magazines, job postings, and information about how to get into this field of work.

User Experience Designer

It has become hard to imagine life without digital media. Most people rely on apps, websites, software programs, and other digital products for work, school, communication, shopping, entertainment, and many other activities, and some spend most of their waking hours using these products. For instance, according to the American Academy of Child & Adolescent Psychiatry in 2024, US teens spend up to nine hours per day using digital media. The interaction people have with digital media is sometimes referred to as a user experience (UX), and it is not something that happens at random. Instead, UX designers carefully plan and develop every part of the interaction, from the way the product looks, to the specific way people use it, to the way that experience makes them feel afterward.

At a Glance

Number of Jobs
About 222,600*

Pay
About $98,000 for 2024*

Educational Requirements
Design skills, fluency in digital design applications

Personal Qualities
Empathy, communication, creativity, problem-solving

Working Conditions
Remote work is common

Future Job Outlook
Growth of 8 percent through 2033*

* For web developers and digital designers

What Does a UX Designer Do?

UX designers strive to make products or services as enjoyable, usable, and accessible as possible. Some work with physical products; however, the term generally refers to digital interfaces. For example, UX designers make websites and apps easy to navigate, intuitive, and fun to use. Other types of digital products that UX designers work with include watches and other wearable technology, health care and government portals, virtual reality experiences, online learning platforms, and interfaces for home appliances and cars.

To create enjoyable, usable, and accessible products, UX designers need to understand how and why people use a specific product. UX designer Saranya Gunasekaran compares the research and planning involved to the process of constructing a house. She says, "Imagine you were building a house. You wouldn't start construction without understanding who will live there, right? In the same way, I design digital products to meet people's needs."[36] In order to know how to meet people's needs, UX designers carry out research and analysis. There are many ways to research users' wants and needs. A designer might interview product users or hold focus groups, in which a small group of people talk about their experiences with the product. They can also survey users' opinions or conduct usability testing, which entails observing how people interact with a product.

Next, UX designers analyze their research data and come up with ideas for improving the design of a product. After that, they employ their design skills to create a wireframe, which is a simplified outline of a proposed web page or application design. In addition, they often create a prototype—or usable model—of their design. They can use that prototype to carry out further research and testing to see whether the new design works well or whether further changes are needed.

A Typical Workday

Trina Moore Pervall is a UX designer and UX researcher. Like many people who work in this field, she explains that her days are always different but usually involve some combination of research and analysis, design work, and meetings with team members or customers. She says, "Some days, I have back-to-back meetings: internal meetings, customer meetings, presentations, or user engagement sessions. Other days, I'm at my desk most of the day: analyzing findings, working on plans for user engagement, creating . . . mockups, or providing guidance to the developers as they commit designs to code."[37]

Many UX designers say that one of the things they enjoy about this job is the way that they can positively impact the lives of other people. Chelsea Singer, a senior UX content designer for Indeed Design, says, "I was intrigued by UX because it offered an opportunity to use information and design to help people achieve a task and take a bit of frustration out of their day." She explains that while the small daily frustrations associated with imperfectly designed products might seem relatively inconsequential, they can have a substantial negative impact on people's lives. She says, "Those moments of frustration don't exist in isolation—they can affect your mood, your day, and how you interact with others (been there). I figured that if I could help alleviate some of this by making the online world a little friendlier, that was something I wanted to get behind."[38]

Education and Training

UX designers have at least a high school diploma, but many possess a bachelor's degree or a higher-level degree in a field like computer science, programming, or graphic design. Some UX designers take shorter types of courses like boot camps or certificate programs at tech schools, where they learn specific UX design skills like wireframing, usability testing, and prototyping.

To work in this field, it is also important to gain experience. Students can do this through internships, which provide numerous career benefits. Job search website Indeed advises, "If you attend college, try to complete an internship program before you graduate or right afterward. Interning can help you learn how to apply UX skills in a professional environment. You can also de-

Designing with People, for People

"I like to define myself as a passionate UX Designer who aims to build meaningful, usable, and accessible products or services. I'm interested in the design process that forms the final result and in how things work. I believe that the best solution is designed with people, not only for people. . . . What I enjoy the most about my work as a UX Designer is having the opportunity to get close to the end-users to understand their needs and design experiences that are meaningful and accessible to them."

—Edoardo Fusaro, senior UX designer for IKEA

Quoted in Maria Myre, "A Day in the Life of a UX Designer: Edoardo Fusaro," Designlab, February 7, 2022. https://designlab.com.

velop valuable connections with others in the industry, which can help you find a job once you graduate."[39] Working on personal projects is another way to gain experience.

By completing UX design projects, designers can build a portfolio, which is essential for working in this field. A portfolio is a collection of real design projects that showcase the skills of the UX designer to potential employers. General Assembly, a school that offers UX design boot camps, explains that the UX job market can be competitive, making a portfolio an important part of finding a job. The school's website states, "Your portfolio serves as a critical tool for landing job interviews and advancing your career. It's more than just a collection of your work—it's a reflection of your design process, problem-solving abilities, and creative flair. A well-crafted portfolio can set you apart from other candidates and open doors to new opportunities."[40]

Skills and Personality

Because UX design involves solving challenges—such as how to make a product attractive and easy to use—creativity, critical

Learning to Navigate Constraints

"The most challenging aspect of my work is navigating constraints. Product managers want to deliver business impact, engineers care about feasibility and implementation time, and UXers are caught in the middle trying to provide a desirable and useful product to users. At the end of the day, users won't know what constraints we face; they simply want to use the product the way they want. . . . Our job as designers is to make sure we meet their needs."

—Konrad Marzec, former UX designer at Indeed

Quoted in Indeed Design Team, "What I Wish I Knew Before Starting a Career in UX Design," Indeed, June 2023. https://indeed.design.

thinking, and problem-solving skills are all beneficial. Empathy is also crucial to success in this field. Twitter cofounder Jack Dorsey is often quoted as succinctly stating, "If you want to build a product that's relevant to people, you need to put yourself in their shoes."[41]

Robert Mayer, a product designer at Netflix, stresses that UX designers must also become comfortable discussing their ideas with other people. He says, "As a designer, presentation skill is a must. You would be always presenting something to someone: a stakeholder presentation of your design solution, or a design review with your peers, even handing off design to developers would require some kind of presentation on your end. Some folks can find this very stressful. You got to overcome your own introversion."[42]

Finally, design is a major part of this job, so UX designers need design skills. UX designer Jane Li explains, "A big part of the job is communicating ideas through visuals. Therefore, knowing the basic design standards and showing well-rounded skills are essential to success as a UX designer."[43] Most UX designers use digital design applications like Figma, Sketch, and Adobe XD to create their designs.

Workplace, Employers, and Pay

Some UX designers work in an office, while others work remotely. Even though user interface design requires a lot of time spent building and testing on a computer alone, many projects are collaborative efforts. UX designers may work with product designers, advertising specialists, web designers, and graphic designers to bring products to the market. They may also need to meet with clients. Good communication skills are therefore needed, as well as the ability to work well as part of a team. UX design lead Stephanie Hagadorn says, "So much of the job isn't about the screen. It's all the conversations, planning, strategy, and relationships along the way that matter. An orchestra of effort from cross-discipline people and teams culminates in what's eventually good design for the user."[44]

According to Bureau of Labor Statistics (BLS) data, the average salary for web and digital interface designers—which includes UX designers—is about $98,000. Top-paying industries include finance and insurance, followed by computer design. UX designers working in advertising and retail may earn less.

What Is the Future Outlook for UX Designers?

Society is very dependent on digital products, and the growth outlook for this job field is positive. The BLS predicts that jobs for digital designers will grow by 8 percent through 2033, with approximately 16,500 job openings each year. This is double the average US job growth rate. The bureau explains that much of this increase is driven by the expansion of e-commerce, which creates a demand for more and more online products and services. The BLS adds, "The continued use of mobile devices to search the web is expected to generate demand for . . . digital designers to create websites and interfaces that work on mobile devices with many different screen sizes."[45]

Find Out More

American Institute of Graphic Arts

www.aiga.org

The American Institute of Graphic Arts is a professional design organization with thousands of members. Its website contains information about design events and competitions. It also houses a variety of educational resources.

Interaction Design Association (IXDA)

https://ixda.org

This organization supports the field of interaction design. Its website has articles, videos, and podcasts. There is also a job board and links to local IXDA groups.

User Experience Professionals Association International

https://uxpa.org

The User Experience Professionals Association International facilitates global education and networking within this field. Its website has an education center that contains information about UX design, professional standards of conduct, and advice on how to get started in the field.

Clinical Pharmacologist

When she was still in school, Lynne knew that she was interested in the medical field, but she did not want to become a doctor. She says, "I was very interested in health and disease but I didn't want to go into medicine and work with patients directly." Instead, she turned to clinical pharmacology. Now, rather than providing primary care for patients directly, she improves their quality of life by developing drugs to treat their illnesses and keep them healthy. Lynne works at the Association of the British Pharmaceutical Industry and enjoys her job a lot. She says, "I really like the idea . . . that every little experiment that I do and data I generate could contribute to helping improve peoples' lives."[46]

At a Glance

Number of Jobs
About 146,600*

Pay
About $100,000 in 2024*

Educational Requirements
Most have a PhD or a medical degree

Personal Qualities
Critical thinking, problem-solving, observation, communication

Working Conditions
In research laboratories and offices as well as hospitals and other health care facilities

Future Job Outlook
Growth of 11 percent though 2033*

* For all medical scientists

What Does a Clinical Pharmacologist Do?

Clinical pharmacologists research and analyze how drugs work in people's bodies so that they can develop effective medical treatments. To do this, they study drug interactions in laboratories, research new drugs, design clinical trials for drugs, develop guidelines for drug usage, and investigate adverse drug reactions.

The American Society for Clinical Pharmacology & Therapeutics describes clinical pharmacologists as a combination of physicians, pharmacists, and scientists. The organization explains that this type of work has a long history, stating, "Clinical Pharmacology, in theory, has been practiced for centuries through observing the effects of herbal remedies and early drugs on humans. Most of this work was done through trial and error."[47] Today, however, technological advances let pharmacologists carry out much more complex research. For example, some clinical pharmacologists utilize genetics to understand how people's genes affect their response to drugs. This allows pharmacologists to personalize drug treatments for individual patients.

While some clinical pharmacologists focus on research, others work directly with patients. Within this field it is also common to specialize in a subfield. For example, toxicology is the study of chemicals that can have adverse effects on people, and neuropharmacology examines how drugs affect the brain and nervous system. No matter what their subfield, most clinical pharmacologists say that their jobs are always interesting and challenging. Clinical pharmacologist Rachel Forfar says, "We try to develop drugs for unmet medical needs that are often overlooked by the pharmaceutical industry, such as developing new antibiotics. I like the challenge of looking at a range of different potential drugs and tests. No day is ever the same and I am constantly learning new techniques and new biology."[48]

A Typical Workday

A clinical pharmacologist who interacts with patients is often part of a team of health care workers. The team might specialize in handling infectious diseases or treating long-term maladies such as cardiovascular disease. The clinical pharmacologist's role on the team may include meeting with an ailing patient to decide on an appropriate drug therapy. The pharmacologist might also

A Field with Many Specializations

"Clinical pharmacology is the best job in the NHS [National Health Service]. I can answer my own research questions while improving patient care! There is room for all interests in clinical pharmacology; from treating people who have been poisoned, to ensuring patients are on the right treatments, through to laboratory research; there is no reason why you can't try it all!"

—Emma Morrison, clinical pharmacologist for the National Health Service in the United Kingdom

Emma Morrison, "What Is It like Being a Pharmacologist?," British Pharmacological Society, 2025. www.bps.ac.uk.

spend part of the day conducting analysis to understand any adverse drug reactions in the patient. Whatever the outcomes of a drug treatment, pharmacologists must spend part of their day detailing their findings in reports. Such documentation is critical to the health records of each patient as well as to the general usefulness of a drug as a treatment.

Those clinical pharmacologists who do not work directly with patients are often researching drugs and their impacts in a laboratory or office. Lynne, for instance, works in a research laboratory. She says, "Most days are spent in the lab using cell and tissue cultures to look at the effect of drug targets. I analyse the data and write up my notes in my lab book. I present my findings at group meetings." She emphasizes that, despite not working with patients, her work includes a lot of interaction and collaboration with other people. She says:

> About 60% of my time is working on my own and 40% working with other people. But when I say working on my own I don't mean locked in a room all by yourself, the labs are open plan so there's always other people about that

you can chat to and ask for help or advice about something. . . . It's a team environment even though you have your individual projects. Working in the lab is really sociable as there are lots of other people to chat to and the radio is always playing.[49]

When not performing lab work or connecting with patients, many clinical pharmacologists turn their interest in research into publishable journal articles to explain their findings to colleagues around the world. They might share these at conferences. By sharing their findings, they allow other researchers to replicate their work and build on it, which leads to the advancement of medical knowledge and improved care of patients.

Education and Training

Most people with a career in pharmacology are well educated. They often start with a bachelor's degree in biology, chemistry, or pharmacology and then move on to earn a PhD. However, some clinical pharmacologists pursue medical degrees instead of or in addition to a PhD. Clinical pharmacologists who work as researchers do not need any special licenses, but those who treat patients need a medical license. In addition to years of education, clinical pharmacologists need to spend a lot of time training. Those who earn a medical degree complete a residency, which is a period spent working in a doctor's office or a hospital. Those who pursue a PhD will usually be involved in extensive research as part of their educational program.

Pharmacologist Ankush Kumar Jha, who specializes in obesity and diabetes, remembers the hard work involved in pursuing his master's degree. He says, "Though I was working tirelessly in the lab (day and night), I was enjoying my master's work. I never thought about relaxing or sleeping or taking time out for fun. I just wanted to finish my work and come up with good results. I finally

While some clinical pharmacologists interact with patients, others do research on drugs and their impacts. In a research laboratory, these professionals analyze cell and tissue cultures to determine the effects of various drugs.

did it and submitted my thesis."[50] One benefit of acquiring that research experience is being able to help train others working in the same laboratory.

Skills and Personality

Critical thinking, curiosity, and observational skills are all important for this career. These skills help clinical pharmacologists design, carry out, and evaluate research effectively. People who work in clinical pharmacology also need strong communication skills so that they can explain their findings to nontechnical audiences or even other staffers. Patience and emotional resilience can also be helpful. Clinical research can take a lot of trial and error and involve unexpected setbacks

Helping the Most People

"I realized that, as a clinical pharmacologist and epidemiologist, if I focused on accelerating drug development, I could potentially improve outcomes for far more patients through advancements in medical science. It wasn't just about treating patients one at a time, it was about addressing global health challenges at scale, particularly in the realm of drug development and regulatory science. The opportunity to influence policy, streamline clinical trials, and accelerate therapeutic innovations motivated me to take this path."

—Klaus Romero, clinical pharmacologist at the Critical Path Institute

Quoted in C-Path Communications, "From Musician to Physician to Clinical Scientist: C-Path CEO Klaus Romero Shares His Journey During National Physicians Week," March 27, 2025. https://c-path.org.

and challenges. Perseverance can help researchers cope with these frustrations and uncertainties.

When asked what skills are most important, clinical pharmacologist Lucy Lee explains that this role requires a combination of technical and personal skills. She says, "A student should work to develop 1) a solid scientific foundation in his/her area of concentration, 2) confidence in questioning and problem-solving abilities, 3) great communications skills in both speaking and writing, especially to explain complex ideas in a simplified manner, and 4) leadership skills."[51]

Workplace, Employers, and Pay

Clinical pharmacologists who conduct research typically work in a laboratory or office. Those who work with patients generally serve in hospitals or other types of health care facilities. However, pharmacologists can be found in many institutions. Some, for example, teach and do research at universities. Others work directly in the drug industry, and more than a few conduct research for the government. According to the Bureau of Labor Statistics (BLS), 34 percent of medical scientists (which includes clinical pharmacologists) work in research and development, 22 percent in hospitals, 13 percent in colleges and universities, 6 percent in medical and diagnostic laboratories, and 4 percent in the pharmaceutical industry.

According to the BLS, the median annual salary for this job is about $100,000. The agency finds that clinical pharmacologists who work in research or pharmaceutical manufacturing tend to earn the highest salaries, while those who work in laboratories or hospitals often receive a somewhat lower salary. Positions at colleges and universities are typically the lowest paying, according to BLS statistics.

What Is the Future Outlook for Clinical Pharmacologists?

Clinical pharmacologists are critical to the development of the drugs that people require to cope with medical conditions. According to research from the Centers for Disease Control and Prevention, about half of Americans take prescription medication, ensuring a continuing need for pharmacologists. The BLS predicts strong future job growth for all medical science careers. As the population ages, there will be an increased need for clinical pharmacologists and medical scientists to create treatments for chronic disease and other health problems. The BLS states, "These scientists will be needed for research into treating diseases, such as Alzheimer's disease and cancer, and problems related to treatment, such as resistance to antibiotics. In addition, medical scientists will continue to be needed for medical research as a growing population travels globally and facilitates the spread of diseases."[52] Overall, the BLS predicts 11 percent job growth in the medical sciences through 2033, which is much faster than the average US job growth rate of 4 percent.

Find Out More

American Society for Clinical Pharmacology & Therapeutics (ASCPT)

www.ascpt.org

The ASCPT is a professional organization that works to advance this field of pharmacology. In addition to information detailing this career, its website provides current news from this field and a job center with open listings and a free résumé review service.

American Society for Pharmacology and Experimental Therapeutics

www.aspet.org

The American Society for Pharmacology and Experimental Therapeutics is a scientific organization that aims to accelerate the development of drugs that will benefit society. Its website has information about pharmacology—including its history—TEDx Talks by members, and a career center.

Society of Toxicology

www.toxicology.org

This professional organization represents people who work in toxicology. Its website has a variety of toxicology resources, including information about the field, its work, and its ethics. There is also a career center that provides information about job opportunities.

Source Notes

Introduction: The Importance of Research and Analysis

1. Prahlada N. Basavanthappa, "Advancing Knowledge and Society: The Crucial Role of Research and Its Dissemination," *Journal of Dr. YSR University of Health Sciences* 13 no. 1, 2024. https://journals.lww.com.
2. World Economic Forum, *Future of Jobs Report 2025*. World Economic Forum, 2025, p. 6.

Data Scientist

3. New York Institute of Technology, "Industry-Specific Applications of Data Science," February 22, 2024. https://online.nyit.edu.
4. Xaltius, "The Rise of the Data Detectives: Unlocking the Secrets of the World with Data Science," Medium, January 16, 2024. https://medium.com.
5. Egor Howell, "Behind the Scenes: Explaining My Work as a Data Scientist," Medium, May 24, 2024. https://medium.com.
6. Bureau of Labor Statistics, "Data Scientists," April 18, 2025. www.bls.gov.
7. Quoted in Oracle Careers Editorial Team, "Data Science at Oracle: A Thriving Career Path," *Oracle Careers Blog*, January 18, 2024. https://blogs.oracle.com.
8. Bureau of Labor Statistics, "Data Scientists."

Financial Analyst

9. Fidelity, "Understanding the Basics of Investing," October 1, 2024. www.fidelity.com.
10. Institute of Management Accountants, "Financial Analyst." www.imanet.org.
11. Quoted in Canada Dough, "A Day in the Life of a Canadian Tire Financial Analyst," Medium, September 12, 2020. https://medium.com.
12. Quoted in Sarah Butcher, "Day in the Life, Pam Chang, Analyst, Citadel Global Equities, Chicago," eFinancialCareers, September 1, 2022. www.efinancialcareers.com.

13. Association for Financial Professionals, "Boost Your Financial Analysis Skills with These 4 Tips," July 29, 2024. www.afponline.org.
14. Association for Financial Professionals, "Top 5 Tasks of a Financial Analyst," February 17, 2023. www.afponline.org.
15. Olu Sonola, "Thinking of a Career as an Economist? Here's My Story," CFA Institute, April 8, 2025. www.cfainstitute.org.
16. Bureau of Labor Statistics, "Financial Analysts," April 18, 2025. www.bls.gov.

Wildlife Biologist

17. Quoted in Interview Portal, "Wildlife Biologist Interview," June 23, 2023. https://theinterviewportal.com.
18. Matt Lau, "Scientist Profile: Matt Lau, Wildlife Biologist," National Park Service, July 8, 2022. www.nps.gov.
19. Lauren McPherson, "So, You Want to Be a Wildlife Biologist?," Maine Department of Inland Fisheries & Wildlife, March 17, 2023. www.maine.gov.
20. Stephanie Manka, "Becoming a Wildlife Biologist: FAQs Answered by a Wildlife Biologist," Fancy Scientist, October 14, 2020. https://stephanieschuttler.com.
21. McPherson, "So, You Want to Be a Wildlife Biologist?"
22. Lau, "Scientist Profile."
23. US Forest Service, "Careers in Wildlife Biology." www.fs.usda.gov.
24. Bureau of Labor Statistics, "Zoologists and Wildlife Biologists," April 18, 2025. www.bls.gov.

Forensic Science Technician

25. National Institute of Justice, "Crime Scene and DNA Basics for Forensic Analysts: Types of Evidence," June 15, 2023. https://nij.ojp.gov.
26. Quoted in Elena Ferrarin, "Antoinette T. Campbell on the Lack of Diversity in Forensic Science—and What She's Doing to Help Change That," *True Crime Blog*, A&E, February 7, 2022. www.aetv.com.
27. Rebecca Learned, "A Forensic Scientist's Path: What a Long, Rewarding Trip It's Been," Association for Women in Science, 2024. https://awis.org.

28. Quoted in Mariana Lozovanu, “Unraveling Mysteries: The Role of Forensic Science in Conservation and Criminal Justice,” Arizona State University, December 17, 2024. https://news.asu.edu.
29. Bureau of Labor Statistics, “Forensic Science Technicians,” April 18, 2025. www.bls.gov.
30. UC Davis Forensic Science Graduate Program, “Career Outlook: Strong Career Opportunities for Forensic Science Graduates,” October 17, 2024. https://forensicscience.ucdavis.edu.
31. Michael Howard, “A Forensic Scientist Talks About the Job,” All Criminal Justice Schools, July 6, 2001. www.allcriminaljusticeschools.com.
32. Howard, “A Forensic Scientist Talks About the Job.”
33. Quoted in Melissa T. Miller, “Reality vs. Hollywood: Forensic Science,” Fleet Science Center, September 25, 2020. www.fleetscience.org.
34. Quoted in Lozovanu, “Unraveling Mysteries.”
35. Bureau of Labor Statistics, “Forensic Science Technicians.”

User Experience Designer

36. Saranya Gunasekaran, “Explaining UX Design Through the Lens of Construction,” UX Matters, March 17, 2025. www.uxmatters.com.
37. Trina Moore Pervall, “A Day in My Life as a UX Designer,” Medium, November 15, 2021. https://medium.com.
38. Quoted in Indeed Design Team, “What I Wish I Knew Before I Became a UX Content Designer,” Indeed Design, 2023. https://indeed.design.
39. Indeed Editorial Team, “How to Get Hired as a UX Designer (Plus Definition and Tips),” Indeed, March 26, 2025. www.indeed.com.
40. General Assembly, “How to Make a UX Design Portfolio That Stands Out: A Complete Guide,” May 17, 2024. https://generalassemb.ly.
41. Quoted in Interaction Design Foundation, “Empathize in UX/UI Design.” www.interaction-design.org.
42. Robert Mayer, “Why You Shouldn’t Become a UX Designer,” UX Planet, June 3, 2022. https://uxplanet.org.

43. Jane Li, “Journey of a UX Designer: The Past, Present and Future of My UX Career,” Medium, December 7, 2023. https://medium.com.
44. Quoted in Indeed Design Team, “What I Wish I Knew Before Starting a Career in UX Design,” Indeed Design, 2023. https://indeed.design.
45. Bureau of Labor Statistics, “Web Developers and Digital Designers,” April 18, 2025. www.bls.gov.

Clinical Pharmacologist

46. Lynne, “Pharmacologist,” Association of the British Pharmaceutical Industry, September 20, 2023. www.abpi.org.uk.
47. American Society for Clinical Pharmacology & Therapeutics, “What Is Clinical Pharmacology?,” 2025. www.ascpt.org.
48. Quoted in British Pharmacological Society, “What Is It like Being a Pharmacologist?,” 2025. www.bps.ac.uk.
49. Lynne, “Pharmacologist.”
50. Quoted in Shyam Krishnamurthy, “Pharmacologist Interview,” Interview Portal, March 3, 2023. https://theinterviewportal.com.
51. Quoted in American College of Clinical Pharmacology, “Ask the Expert Interviews.” https://accp1.org.
52. Bureau of Labor Statistics, “Medical Scientists,” April 18, 2025. www.bls.gov.

Interview with a UX Designer

Wes Biffar is an award-winning interactive art director and user interface (UI)/user experience (UX) designer. (UI design is related to UX design, but is more focused on the look and feel of a product rather than the overall experience of the user.) He has worked in the business for more than twenty years. His experience ranges from theatrical marketing, to e-commerce, to consumer product design. This interview was done by email.

Q: Why did you become a UX designer?

A: I kind of fell into this role. Initially I wanted to be a photographer and began pursuing that, but—while I am still passionate about photography—I realized I really enjoyed laying out my photos and content and creating designs. So, I switched gears and ended up becoming a designer.

It was really the UI (User Interface) aspect that first drew me into this career. I'd say I still lean more towards the UI end of things. But UX (User Experience) is really what drives it all and ultimately is the reason for what I do and why I enjoy it.

Q: Can you describe your typical workday?

A: I always start by sitting down and planning out my day. I make a To Do list and use that to keep me on track. My day is divided up by meetings and the actual "work" of designing. Quite often I'll find myself working on multiple projects at once, so there can be a lot of "context switching." The To Do list helps with this. It really depends on where I'm at within a project [that determines] what work I'd be doing during the day.

If it's a new project, I start by creating a User Flow Chart so that I can map out the experience, set the stage, and get a birds-eye-view of how a user might interact with the experience we're crafting.

After User Flows are done and approved, I'd move on to wireframes. These are very rudimentary, low-fidelity, mock-ups of what the experience might look like. Once wireframes are approved, we may move on to testing those with users to see how they react to it. We use that information to refine the designs and fix any issues that may have been discovered.

After that we move on to the Visual Design phase, where we add in the actual content: copy, photography, colors, interactive elements, etc. . . . This is the fun part. The project really starts to come alive. We may do many different versions of layouts as we work through visual solutions for things. We also need to consider different screen sizes [because] the layout will shift and be different on a small device like a cell phone than it will on a desktop viewport.

If we hadn't already tested the design with users during the wireframe phase, we should be doing that after the visual design has been approved. We need to know how users feel about the product we're designing before we spend the time and effort to develop it, only to find out it's not what users want, need, or know how to use.

After everything is tested and we're happy with the design, then it moves on to the development phase, and that team builds it with code.

Obviously, this is not all happening in a day. But that's the process we try to follow. On any typical day I'd be working on one of those aspects.

Q: What do you like most about your job?

A: I like the creativity and problem-solving aspect of the job.

Q: What do you like least about your job?

A: My least favorite thing is the number of meetings and how those meetings break up the day and my concentration from the work I'd like to be doing. Ideally, I'd just sit down and do the work uninterrupted. When you have large blocks of time to do the work, you can get into a "flow state" and work becomes fun, fast, and efficient. When the work gets interrupted by meetings or other things, it can take quite a while to get back into that state.

Q: Is there anything about your job that is not the way you expected it to be?

A: It's not just about the way things "look." It's surprising how much copy (the text used for a web page or product) plays a role. It's probably the most important element in UX.

Q: What personal qualities do you find most valuable for this type of work?

A: Empathy is extremely important as a UI/UX Designer. It's vital to be able to put yourself "in the shoes" of the users. We need to think like they do and try to imagine what they may be going through as they use our product. That's our job in a nutshell.

Q: What advice do you have for students who might be interested in this career?

A: It's a very interesting and fulfilling career. Be empathetic. Always think of the user. Don't focus solely on the visuals—although those are very important as well.

If you're passionate about it and interested, then don't wait. Start doing it on your own. Create some personal projects and learn by doing.

Q: Is there anything else that you think students interested in this field should think about?

A: AI [artificial intelligence] is changing careers at an extremely fast rate. Definitely, get familiar with AI and use it as much as you can to speed up your work and make you more efficient. I use it daily to brainstorm, write copy, answer questions, create imagery, and even create working prototypes! It has become a very useful tool for me.

Other Jobs If You Like Research and Analysis

Actuary
Biostatistician
Climate scientist
Economist
Epidemiologist
Ethical hacker
Food scientist
Forester
Genetic counselor
Geoscientist
Historian
Hydrologist
Informatics nurse
Information security analyst
Landscape architect
Market research analyst
Meteorologist
Operations research analyst
Plant breeder
Policy analyst
Population ecologist
Private investigator
Real estate appraiser
Research assistant
Research librarian
Social researcher
Sports data analyst
Urban planner

Editor's note: The online *Occupational Outlook Handbook* of the US Department of Labor's Bureau of Labor Statistics is an excellent source of information on jobs in hundreds of career fields, including many of those listed here. The *Occupational Outlook Handbook* may be accessed online at www.bls.gov/ooh.

Index

Picture Credits

Cover: PeopleImages/Shutterstock

10: Gorodenkoff/Shutterstock
19: Stockfour/Shutterstock
26: USFWS Photo/Alamy Stock Photo
49: PeopleImages/Shutterstock

About the Author

Andrea C. Nakaya holds a bachelor of arts in English and a master of arts in communications from San Diego State University. She has written and edited hundreds of articles and more than fifty books on current issues. She currently lives in Eagle, Idaho.